T H E
POWER
OF CREDIT
IS
IN YOUR
HANDS

TONY SANTOS

The Power of Credit is in Your Hands is a comprehensive guide to understanding the credit industry and advice on how to establish, repair and rebuild your credit history.

The Power of Credit Publishing © 2015 Tony Santos

ISBN-13: 978-1505823899
ISBN-10:1505823897

The Power of Credit Publishing
Chicago, Illinois
2015

THE
POWER
OF CREDIT
-IS-
IN YOUR
HANDS

TONY SANTOS

THE POWER OF CREDIT
PUBLISHING
POWEROFCREDIT.COM

TONY

CONTENTS

SANTOS

Let's talk about CREDIT!

"...people would be willing to openly talk more about sex and their relationships than they would about credit." -Tony Santos

DEDICATION

I would like to dedicate this book to my wife who has been my best friend and supported me on my many adventures, I love you.

To my kids who love me unconditionally and who I love the same.

My daughter who helped me with the editing of the book and gave great input and perspective, thank you. I'm so proud of you.

To my mom who has always been there for me.

To my family and friends who believed in me even at times I didn't believe in myself.
You know who you are.

Last but not least...

God who through him all things are possible. With him I can be everything and without him
I am nothing.

To the reader I thank you for your time which is precious and we never get back. I hope this book is helpful and informative, as that is its
purpose.

FORWARD

In today's society, credit is the driving force behind many of the decisions made in our lives. It can be the difference between having a home and being homeless, being employed or unemployed, having light and gas services, a car for transportation, and having either financial stability or having financial stress and hardships.

When considering the importance of the fore mentioned, it sounds like credit can be crucial to our way of living. Well if it's as powerful as it seems, wouldn't it be a good idea to know as much as possible about it?

When we consider the impact credit can have on all aspects of our lives it's really shocking that it isn't an everyday topic of discussion. In fact, people would be willing to openly talk more about sex and their relationships than they would about credit. I strongly believe that needs to change.

Hundreds of thousands of people are struggling with damaged credit, delinquent debt, and lack of resources and have no one to talk to about it. It can be because they are embarrassed, or because the lack of knowledge.

No matter the reason, it is a discussion that needs to happen more often. With over 70% of the people in this country living check to check and struggling to pay bills on time, having a stronger support system in place can help so that we can begin to reach our goals. The key to building this support system in my opinion is education.

By educating ourselves on Credit and Financial literacy, we are arming ourselves with the tools needed to fix a problem so many of us are experiencing. They say when you know better you do better. This book was written to give people the opportunity not only to help themselves but to possibly help others.

INTRODUCTION

Before we begin,

I would like to first and foremost congratulate you on selecting this book to read. By doing so, you have already separated yourself from the masses; you are now one of the few people who will know and understand the depth and meaning behind the word **Credit**.

I wrote this book for several reasons but the first reason among them is so that I can empower you. By reading this book you will receive knowledge of one of the world's best kept secrets: Credit. It is my sincere hope that after reading this book your life will change for the better. That hope brings me to the second reason I wrote this book: I want to make a difference. Through my years of experience, I have seen firsthand how credit impacts people's lives; in both good and bad ways. Thus I have been led to have the desire to make a difference in this world before I leave it and I believe can do this through credit.

It is my sincere plea that you readers take what you are reading and soak it in; be the most absorbent sponge that you can be because the information within these pages will greatly benefit you.

Take this knowledge, **learn it, understand it, use it**, and then **pass it** on to the next person. Knowledge is power and the power is now in your hands; make a positive impact with this power. Change your world or the world. Understand that credit is a power that runs as deep as oceans and once you can understand and control your credit, any "waves" sent your way will not capsize your life.

I hope that this book enlightens, educates, and inspires you to do what you can to take control of your credit and your financial future.

Thank You,
Tony Santos

THE CLASS THAT WAS NEVER TAUGHT

AS I read up on and studied credit and learned the importance and value of it, I found myself asking **"Why was this never taught in school?"**

I have met numerous people from all walks of life and from different educational backgrounds and when I asked if they ever learned about credit in school, the majority of these people said "NO." I've had clients who were doctors, lawyers, and even a professor or two and I was surprised to find that their knowledge of credit was average at best. Once I realized that some of the most intelligent people I knew had minimal knowledge of credit, I personally became obsessed with it. I wanted to know everything about the subject because it was something that was never taught.

Why exactly was credit never taught?

Simply because **"THEY"** don't want you to know just how powerful credit is. Think about it. There are trillions of dollars at stake here. For every mistake that you make, somebody is capitalizing and making money off of it. If everyone knew how to work their credit and how to keep their credit respectable, somebody, somewhere, would be losing money because they can no longer benefit from your mistakes and ignorance.

I am setting out to change that. I am going to teach you everything I know about credit. You've opened this book and now you are going to learn some great and valuable information.

So let the classes begin.

BEST KEPT SECRET;
DEEPER THAN THE OCEANS

The entire concept of credit, when you really think about it, is really deep. There are literally strangers exchanging all sorts of information about you with companies full of more strangers; they will analyze the data and decide on how your financial future will unfold and whether you are a **"High Risk"** or not. The concept behind the system is that history will repeat itself; whatever you have done in the past you will most likely do again in the future. Then they will calculate a score to reflect your risk level and turn you into a number. Lenders will then use that number to decide if they want to do business with you and at what cost.

Everything about credit is basically one big secret. Why is that? It is the same reason credit is rarely a topic presented in the classroom. Credit is a big money machine. Lenders love that people do not know much about credit. They like when you damage your credit. It means **higher interest rates** which in turn means more money for them.

It is a trillion dollar money making business so it is no surprise that the workings of credit is a secret. The credit system is so flawed that 1 in every 4 credit reports contains an error on it. That is pretty sad because those errors can cost people thousands of dollars. Why is it so easy to get a negative mark on your report than it is to get a positive one? If you were to pay your light bill on time for ten years, that will not show up on your report. Try missing just one monthly payment and a negative marking will immediately show up on your report.

Credit is used to determine many aspects of your life. Can you get a new car? Will you be able to buy a house? Will this employer hire you? All of these questions are answered by credit yet many people know little to nothing about credit and especially how to benefit from it. I have seen how credit can help people and how it can hurt them. It can either lead to the American Dream or turn into the American Nightmare. By simply picking up this book and reading it, you are now privy to the secret and it is no longer a mystery to you. I often say that credit is deeper than the oceans and if you were to pile up all of the money made off of credit, I promise you it would be able to reach the deepest ocean floor.

SET UP TO FAIL

In the previous chapters you may have noticed I highlighted the word **"They."** When I use the word They, I am referring to the Financial System as a whole. This system includes the **Banks, Financial Institutions** and the (CRA) **Credit Reporting Agencies**. They as a whole have designed, developed and implemented a system that is Set Up for You to Fail. The business of lending money is as big as it gets. There are literally trillions of dollars being exchanged borrowed and made all day everyday all over the world. The banks, financial institutions and credit bureaus all work together hand and hand in this system.

The way this system works is simple. The Banks use your credit rating to determine if they will do business with you and at what interest rate. **The credit bureaus purposely keep your credit score down so that the financial institutions can charge you higher interest rates.**

The higher the interest rate the more money they make off of you. The credit reporting agencies do this because the financial institutions are their biggest clients. How it works is the financial institutions gather all the information they have about you like your name, birthday, address, social security number, accounts history, etc. They give this information about you to the credit bureaus for Free. The credit bureaus use their software to analyze the information and calculate a credit rating which the banks use to determine your risk level. The financial institutions however have to pay to get the information back from the credit bureaus. Being that these financial institutions are the credit bureaus best customers they want these institutions to make money so that they can keep giving them money for the service.

Years ago before the credit reporting agencies existed banks and other lending institutions would have to pay someone to analyze your information to determine if you would be a **Good loan** or a **Bad loan**. Then a software was developed that could do the work for them. What this did was make it so that the banks wouldn't have to pay someone a hefty salary to do this job. So you see the credit bureaus save the banks a lot of money and time with the service that they provide. The idea behind the software that is used is that History will Repeat Itself. This is why they report your Past Payment History. If you paid late in the past then it is more than likely you will pay late again in the future and vice versa if you made your payments on time in the past then chances are you would make your payments on time in the future. With this system in place it made the banks job much easier in deciding who was a good loan or a bad loan. At the end of the day that's all you are to them is a loan. You're either a loan number or a file number. They don't care about you at all. You are just a number with a dollar amount attached to it. So the more money they can make off of you the happier they are.

The credit reporting agencies are one of the biggest tools used by this system to make more money off of you then they should. By hiding the way the system works, by not properly educating consumers on how the system works, by manipulating the scoring system so your credit rating isn't being reported accurately, by purposely keeping your credit score down so that you can be charged higher interest rates. See the system is designed for the financial institutions to get rich and succeed off of your hard work, while you the consumer is set up to fail.

There are so many flaws in the credit reporting system that cost consumers an unmeasurable amount of money. By the credit reporting agencies reporting inaccurate information on your credit report, your credit score drops because of these errors and you end up paying more money then you should for credit based services. Unfortunately this system is all about Creed and making money and consumers are just pawns in the grand scheme of things. I truly want this to change and the only way to bring about this change is to educate ourselves and our children. We need to be educated enough on the topic of credit so that we can change the way things are currently setup. By being able to understand credit and the way it works and why it works the way it does is the key. By structuring our credit files to look exactly how the software wants it to look so we can be given higher credit scores. By monitoring our credit reports and recognizing and catching inaccuracies and errors before it is too late. By avoiding being charged higher interest rates on loans. This will surely help in the process of changing things. In this book we are going to go deep into the credit system and learn **What credit is, Why it is so important,** how credit scores are calculated, the **Do's and Don'ts** of credit and much, much more. I really hope you learn something valuable and take something from this book as this is one of the books main purposes.

BAD CREDIT HURTS

I want to share with you a story that I hope will enlighten you on just how crucial having good credit is. This tale is about a man who we shall just call John. John was your typical guy; he worked hard, had a loving wife, and two kids. After months of searching and applying for employment, John had finally landed a new job as an engineer in a high rise building in the amazing city of Chicago. As you can imagine, John was ecstatic with his new job position.

John, however, like all humans, had a few flaws, especially when it came to paying attention to really important things, like his credit. As a student in high school and then later in college, John had the tendency to sometimes zone out during class lectures. One such class lecture (economics and consumer ed.) dealt with finances. John never truly paid attention to lectures in class and as such he never really paid attention to his own financial decisions.

Little did John know that his class time naps would come back to haunt him in the future.

John is now a working class adult with a family he loves, and it is his desire to give them the American Dream. However, after missing a couple of credit card payments here and there and having a couple of unpaid cell phone and medical bills, John's credit score was as low as his economics grade in high school (that is, it was really low). John figured that since he finally landed a good job, it was time to upgrade his lemon and get him a shiny new car. After a couple of months of working hard, he was able to save up enough money to put a down payment on a new car. John entered the car dealership filled with anticipation and excitement, that is, until he saw the appallingly high interest rate he would be paying. With a credit score of only 590, John was staring down an outrageous interest rate of 19%. As we continue with this story, I want you to remember that **you cannot run from your credit**; it will always come back to haunt you.

Continuing with our story, John leaves the dealership in his new car and all is well for now. Not long after, John begins receiving credit card offers in the mail and eventually falls prey to (I mean accepts the offer of) the lender and applies for a card. Upon being approved at an 18.8% interest rate, he now possesses the "Power of The Plastic". A few more months pass and things are continuing to go well; the job is awesome, he loves his car, and all of his credit cards are being paid on time. Therefore, John believes that it would be a great idea to invest in a home for his family. So John repeats the cycle and after some time he is able to save up enough for a down payment on a house. At this point, John's credit score has improved, but with the high debt of the car loan and credit cards weighing on it, his score is still not where it should be. This does not deter John, however, and he eventually makes a down payment on a new house. Unfortunately, after the initial down payment and closing costs, John's bank account is literally empty.

Eighteen months have passed and John is seemingly living the American Dream. He has a nice car, a beautiful house, credit cards, a great job, and a loving family. Things couldn't be better. But little did John know that the **American Dream could quickly turn into the American Nightmare.** As such things go, the company John was working for experienced some heavy financial losses and had to cut back on expenses; John was one of those expenses. The loss of his job was a heavy blow to John; how was he to provide for his family and pay his bills without a job? He tried for months to get another job, but with the economy being in such a terrible state, he had no success. With no job, no savings, and not many choices, John began to use his credit cards for everyday expenses such as food and utilities and he was unable to make the payments on those credit cards, his car, or the house. The car was eventually repossessed since John was no longer making payments on the **secured loan**. His house eventually went into foreclosure because he could no longer afford to pay the mortgage. Now to add insult to injury, John snapped under the pressure of his financial hardships; his entire persona changed. He became depressed, stressed out and extremely unhappy. This mindset started to take a toll on John's health, his relationship with his wife and with his kids. John was in worst shape financially then he had ever been in his life.

This story may seem a little drastic or depressing to some, but the message is clear. John's credit played a major role in his life and eventually led to his downfall. If he'd taken more care of his credit when he was younger, things may certainly have turned out differently. He would have been approved at a lower interest rate for his car loan and would have been able to save money in that regard. The same applies for his credit cards and mortgage. Adding up the extra money he spent on monthly interest rates over the period of time he was paying, John could have saved up a large amount of money to set aside for an emergency fund that would have come in handy after losing his job.

Despite the mistakes that John made, I cannot help but to sympathize with him. There are millions of people who go through similar situations due to a lack of proper education concerning credit and finances. Most people today, especially our youth, are taught little to nothing about credit: how to use it, how it works, and what not to do. A lot of teens are simply handed a credit card and told to go spend it up. After all, they don't have to pay the money back *until later*. This method, however, is just breeding a generation of future Johns who will face a future where debt is a constant part of their lives.

R̶x̶

CREDIT CURES

NOW that I have told you John's tragic story, I would like to share with you another tale; one that you will hopefully find more positive and enlightening.

This story is about a young woman named Claire.

Claire is a hardworking young woman who was taught the value of credit at a young age. Claire's father was a financial advisor and as such he knew the importance of credit and how it could affect one's life. He shared his knowledge with his daughter in the hopes that she would have a bright future; financially and otherwise.

When Claire was in her younger years, she wanted the things that all of her friends desired: the latest fashion, new gadgets, etc. In order to buy all of these things, Claire's father made her work for it by giving her thirty candy bars every week to sell. Claire's father would buy the candy bars for her with the condition that Claire would sell the candy and then pay her father back for the original price of the candy bars at the end of the week and she would keep the profit to buy whatever she wanted.

Claire honored the arrangement and paid her father back every week for a month. Upon seeing that his daughter was being responsible, he increased the number of candy bars that Claire could sell to sixty. Claire once again proved to be reliable and paid her father back every week like clockwork. Eventually Claire started making enough money that she was able to buy her own candy bars.

It wasn't until years later that Claire understood the valuable lesson that such a simple task bestowed; yet she took it with her in life. She graduated high school with commendable grades and attended college with an academic scholarship. After losing her childhood pet to an illness, Claire decided to become a veterinarian and majored in biology and pre-medicine. In order to save up for medical school, Claire started a small business on campus and sold handmade jewelry and other fashion accessories. She decided to apply for a credit card and was approved. Since she knew the value of borrowing and repaying, her credit cards were always paid off on time and kept balances below 30%. So with a positive credit background and her lucrative jewelry making business, Claire decided it was time to buy her very first car (girly squeal of delight from Claire!).

When Claire went to the dealership with her father and her credit was pulled, it was no surprise to her father that his daughter had a great credit score rating of 730. She was easily financed for a new car at a very good interest rate of 3%. Her father couldn't have been more proud of her at that moment.

Fast forward a few years later and Claire has graduated from college and medical school and works at an animal hospital. However, it is Claire's desire to open her own animal hospital and shelter so she eventually goes to a bank to discuss obtaining a business startup loan. Once again her credit is pulled and her report looks great; she had little to no balance on her 3 credit cards, no student loans, and only ten months of payments left on her car loan. Her credit score was an amazing 790 and the banker was quite impressed. Here was a young woman, fresh out of school with not only a degree and a job, but a nearly perfect credit score. She was immediately approved for her startup loan and was able to open her own practice

When asked how she managed to have such great credit, Claire would simply smile and say "Candy bars and a father's love." Indeed it was her father's lessons that allowed Claire to develop the healthy habits that would lead to her even healthier credit score. It is easy to see how Claire's good credit led to many good opportunities. **It is no secret that Knowledge is Power, and we know now that Credit is Power.** So having knowledge of credit is like having a Super Power.

TEACH YOUR CHILDREN

Growing up without being taught the value of credit is a huge setback for many adults. I cannot count the number of times I've heard people lament over their lack of knowledge while in their youth. I've done it myself. It is said that **"when you know better, you do better."** I find this to be very true so I have made it one of my priorities to teach my kids about credit and I urge you to do so too. Teaching your kids about credit, how it works, and why it is important can prevent a lot of stress in the future and can prevent them from making the same mistakes that you and I may have made. I enjoy meeting young adults with blank credit slates. I can then impart my knowledge on them and turn those blank slates into beautiful credit paintings and picture perfect profiles.

I remember when I got my first credit card. I was absolutely ecstatic about the idea of "free money." You mean I could buy all of these new shoes and clothes and

I don't have to pay until later? Awesome, right? More like, wrong, wrong, wrong! I ended up maxing out the card within three hours of getting it and my credit was damaged before I even knew what a credit score was. I always wish someone had shown me the ropes but I cannot change the past. I can only influence the future. Therefore I talk to my children about credit. I have advised my 19 year old daughter on how to get started with building a perfect credit score by opening up a credit card and using it responsibly. God willing she listens, her credit score will be perfect by the time she is 21 and creditors would love to do business with her. She now knows the importance of credit and if she wishes to buy a new car, get a home, and start a family someday she will know how credit can impact all of that.

If you begin teaching your kids the value of credit now, you will pave a smooth road to success for them. Structuring a perfect credit file isn't difficult when you are starting with a blank file. It's after you mess it up that it becomes a challenge. A blank file can reach a 700+ credit score within 90 days if you do things the proper way. If you simply open two credit cards and make sure you follow the advice given in this book, your credit score can skyrocket.

I cannot stress it enough the value of teaching your kids about credit. Credit is truly a secret to success and what loving parent doesn't want their kid to be successful? Teach your child the knowledge that you have gained in this book and share with them your experiences. Teach them how to read a credit report, how to manage their money, balance check books, how to open a bank account. Break the cycle of ignorance and plant the seeds of success, knowledge and greatness. As your child matures into an adult you will see the benefits of your efforts and watch the seed you planted grow into a money tree. You can save your kid not only money, but stress, debt, heartache and pain as well. The children are our future, so let's ensure that it is a bright and debt free future.

WHAT IS CREDIT?
Why Is It So Important?

Credit is technically defined as:

"The ability of a customer to obtain goods or services before payment, based on the trust that payment will be made in the future."

Seems pretty straightforward, right? Well what I would like to tell you is that credit is so much more. In today's society, a person's credit is one of the most important determining factors of said person's future. Credit gives you the power of Choice and Trust. Credit is money; it opens up your options and gives you better choices. Having good credit allows for bigger purchases such as a home or new car with the added benefit of not needing to have all of the money upfront. There are many more definitions, explanations, and interpretations of the word "credit" but I am not going to bore you with those. The main idea here is that credit is important! I will reiterate that throughout this book so that you do not forget.

Credit can provide financial stability and be a dream come true; or, it can be a nightmare and lead to financial stress and hardship. I have met many people and have heard countless tales of how credit has improved or ruined their lives. Why does credit impact our lives so strongly, and why do many of us feel helpless when it comes to credit? The answer is simple. We do not know and understand what credit is and therein lies a big problem. Therefore, I will begin with a simple lesson.

There are three major credit bureaus that gather information about you from the different lenders you have dealt with, and these bureaus provide one free annual credit report per bureau: **Experian, Equifax, and TransUnion also known as CRAs, or Credit Reporting Agencies**, use software to generate what is called a **FICO Score**. Your FICO Score, in a nutshell, is what tells lenders if you are credit-worthy and trustworthy or not. The higher the score, the easier it would be for you to qualify for loans; the lower your score, the harder it would be to qualify for loans. If you do happen to qualify, the interest rates would be significantly higher. As an example, a FICO Score of 720 or above is considered to be a good score and a score of 620 or below is typically considered a bad score.

There are five components used to generate your FICO Score. They are as follows, in order of importance:

1. Payment History - When you make payments to a lender, most of them report to CRAs how you made those payments, when those payments were made, and how much you paid. It is important that you make your payments on time as your payment history accounts for **35% of your score.**

2. Debt/Utilization Rate - CRAs look to see how much credit you have available and how much of that available credit you have already used. This is to observe whether or not you abuse or take advantage of the amount of credit that you have. To maximize the amount of points you may receive per reporting period, you want your utilization rate to be at or **below 30%** of your available credit. If you have $10,000 in available credit, you should only have about $3,000 of that used. It is important to monitor how much of your credit you use as this can save you money on your account's interest rates. **Debt/ Utilization Rate accounts for 30% of your FICO Score.**

3. Length of History - This is how long you have had a credit background. The longer you have had credit, the better. To put this in perspective, if you had an account for ten years and you make your payments on time, this exemplifies that you can be trusted long term. This factor makes up **15% of your score.**

4. New Credit - CRAs take notice of how often you open up a new account and when. If you have opened multiple new accounts in a short period of time, this can be seen as a sign of irresponsibility or as a lack of money management skills. It is vital that you open up new accounts for good reasons as this adds variety to your account; however, make sure to use caution and responsibility when doing so. This factor makes up **10% of your FICO Score.**

5. Variety - Lenders and CRAs love to see variety on your report. They like to know that you can be trusted to pay for different things in different ways. Therefore, you typically want to have 1 installment loan and 2 or 3 revolving accounts. This counts as the last **10% of your FICO Score.**

Now that you have a basic understanding of what credit is and how it is perceived and calculated, let's continue empowering ourselves with the knowledge of credit. Today, credit is carefully scrutinized more than ever before. Even employers are now checking the credit score and history of applicants and having a good credit background can be the difference between landing that dream job and being in the unemployment line. It is also no secret that credit can affect your search for a home or an apartment. Most renters now check the credit background of prospective residents to help make a decision of whether or not to rent to them. Credit is also a major deciding factor for lenders when considering an applicant for a loan. They use your credit background and score to determine if you qualify for any loan programs and at what interest rates.

Let me share an example of just how critically important **1 point** on an interest rate can be. The difference between mortgages of $200,000 at a 30 year fixed interest rate of 4% versus the same mortgage at a fixed interest rate of 5%, can be approximately $50,000 over the life of the loan. So you see, having a good credit score can really impact you in a lot of positive ways and vice versa.

By picking up this book you are benefitting yourself greatly and for that I am truly proud of you. However, this is only the beginning and things have yet to even get interesting. With that being said, grab a pen and a piece of paper (or your smartphone for you tech-savvy people), and prepare to take down some key points and notes. We haven't even gotten to the fun stuff yet!

How to Read a Credit Report

NOW the real lessons begin. We know how and why credit is important, and we have seen some real world examples of the impact of credit. Now it's time for a lesson on how to read your credit report. Sure you now know some new things from the previous chapters, but how do you even find out how good or bad your credit is? How can you tell it's good or bad and why is it good or bad? Learning how to decipher and understand your credit report will help you to answer these questions.

If it is your first time looking at a credit report, you can easily become quite confused. Honestly the first time I saw mine, the only thing I understood and recognized was my name! The first thing to understand is that since there are three CRAs, there are three physically different looking credit reports. Although you can request a blended report with all three agencies on it, it is helpful to know that individual credit reports from the three different agencies are fundamentally similar in some aspects. Understanding how to read these reports is going to be absolutely essential in order for you to use the tools and tips that I am going to share with you later. Therefore the goal here is to help you to be able to read any report from any of the agencies.

The first bit of information you will come to is your **Identity** or **Personal Information**. As its title/headline states, this is detailed information about you; name, date of birth, current and previous addresses, your employers and employment history, your phone numbers, and of course, your social security number. It is very important that you double check to make sure that all of the information present is true and accurate.

Whereas the Personal Information section was the appetizer of the report, the next section you will encounter is the main course: Your **Credit Accounts**. Here you will find a great deal of information such as:

- The name and address of the Creditor
- Your account number
- The type of account you have (credit card, installment, mortgage, etc.)

- Your most recent outstanding balance
- The date your account was opened
- Whether the account is opened or closed

- If you are paying as agreed and are on time with payments
- If you have been 30, 60, 90, or more than 180 days late for a payment and when
- If the original account was transferred to a Collection Agency, and if so, their contact info
- If the account was charged off
- Month by month payment history dating back up to 12 or more months
- If the report is for a revolving account, then the limit will be displayed.
- If the report is for an installment loan, then the original amount and terms will be detailed.
- If you are solely responsible for the payment

This information is continuously updated and at times may be inaccurate or incorrect. If there are errors then it could be the fault of the original creditor or the CRAs.

After the aforementioned section, you will come to the section that contains your **Public Information**. Here you will find:

- Bankruptcies
- Court Judgments
- Foreclosures
- State and Federal tax liens
- Child support payment orders

Following the Public Information will be the section containing what is called a **Consumer Statement** or **Personal
Statement.** You can use this section to file a statement regarding a dispute on your file that future creditors can access and read. You will then come to the section known
as the **Summary**. Here you will find an all-in-one detailed
look at all of the information on your report.
This will include:

- The total amount of debt, broken down into
  categories
- The total number of open, closed, and delin
  quent accounts
- The total amounts for open and/or closed
  delinquent accounts

This gives lenders a quick look into the variety on your account that they like to see.

Finally you will arrive at the section called **Inquiries.**
If anyone requests a current copy of your report, the CRAs
record that on the report. The reason for this, in a nutshell,
is so that lenders can take notice of how often your account has been pulled for an inquiry. The importance of
inquiries will be discussed in the next chapter.

CREDIT FROM THE GROUND UP

SO how exactly do you start building or rebuilding your credit and adding the positives? I am going to tell you how to do so in the next few pages and it is crucial that you follow the steps closely. Not doing so can result in time and money being wasted and lost.

The first thing you should do is to figure out your current finances because you need to know exactly how much money you are bringing in and how much is going out. This is called **Debt to Income Ratio**. Once you have these numbers together, it will be easier to manage your money and bill payments. Just as a reminder, it is important to pay your bills on time because it makes up **35%** of your credit score.

The next step is to **open up a bank account** if you do not already have one; set up both a checking and a savings account. Surprisingly, many people that I have encountered do not have bank accounts because they don't like or trust banks, especially after they have damaged their credit. These people just completely shut down and do not want anything to do with banks. This is due also in part by the fact that some people have the misconception that their debit cards are going to affect their credit. This is not true at all since banks do not report your account activity to the CRAs. Having a bank account is actually very beneficial. It looks good to lenders, it helps to keep your money organized, and if you set up an automatic bill payment system, it will help to keep all of your bills paid on time given that there are adequate funds in your account. Having a bank account is also advantageous because it will give you the opportunity to build a rapport with your banker and any future lenders. You will soon see why this relationship is important.

Now that you have your finances figured out and a bank account set up, it is time to move on to the next step. This step is crucial and going to directly affect your credit.

What you want to do now is open up a **Secured Credit Card.** How this works is pretty simple: put your money into an account and in return your bank will give you a credit card with the same amount on it (notice: usage of this card will be reported to the CRAs). The amount of money you put on the card is dependent upon the type of card. Some cards require a minimum payment of $200 and allow you to put up to $3,000. If you are completely committed to not messing up your credit then I recommend putting as much money as you can towards the card. However, if you are unsure and still a little undecided and not confident, then just put the minimum amount necessary. **Secured Credit Cards are a great way to start building or rebuilding your credit.** All you have to do is use the card and then pay back what you owe monthly. Just be sure to keep the usage down to 30% or below and always make timely payments. The activity and usage of these cards are reported to the credit bureaus and if used in the proper way they can improve your credit score. It is my advice to try to get two Secured Credit Cards if possible. This doubles the positive effects on your credit score when both cards are used properly.

The next tip I have for you is going to be a bit of a shocker but trust me, this is a game changer. This book is **filled with Gems** that I want you to remember and pay close attention to and this is one of them. If possible, get your name put on somebody else's credit card: mom, dad, grandma, your best friend, it doesn't matter as long as they are financially responsible and you would trust them with your savings. When you are put on somebody else's credit card you are becoming an **Authorized User.** This allows the credit history of someone else's account to show up on your credit report. Hopefully you see where I am going here; if grandma has great credit and a beautiful credit history then this will serve to enhance your credit and do wonders for your credit score. For example, if grandma has a $10,000 limit and has only used $1,500, has had the credit card for 10 years, and never missed a payment, adding your name to her account could grant you a credit score boost from 30 to 50 points. This could happen in as little as 30 to 45 days, which is amazing since it usually takes a lot longer to increase your credit score.

This is called **Credit Piggybacking.** Credit Piggybacking is a technique that has been used for years to help boost credit scores and it is one of the few **Secrets of the Trade** that will greatly aid you on your journey to great credit. There are several more benefits of using this technique but I will come back to them later. For now we need to get back to building up your credit from scratch.

This next step can only be taken after you have completed the above steps because this step can only happen after your credit score has increased some. Once your score has improved you should then open an **Unsecured Credit Card.** This is why building a rapport with your banker is a good idea because it is them who will help you to apply and (hopefully) get approved for an Unsecured Credit Card. Getting approved for this card is a good sign that lenders are now willing to deal with and trust you. Therefore, do not be afraid to sit down with your banker and tell them about your credit and financial goals.

The final step is to open up an Installment Loan. This is a loan that is repaid over a set time period with a set number of payments. An example of an **installment loan** is a mortgage or car loan. Many banks have installment loan programs and **Credit Building Programs** that will aid you. Asking your banker for details will prove to be beneficial in the long run. If you are able to open up an installment loan, I suggest that you take whatever amount of money your bank approves you for and put it into an account and set up automatic payments so that you don't have to worry about missing a payment.

If you follow all of the advice outlined in this chapter, I promise you that you will see positive and dramatic changes in your credit and you will be satisfied with the results. Starting over is never easy but the hardest part is getting started. Once you get started you will find that it is not as hard as you first assumed to build up your credit. Don't keep ignoring the issues and putting them off until later. At the end of the day it is your credit that will improve and it is you who will reap the benefits. All I ask of you is that you Decide and Commit. Make the decision to deal with your credit and then commit to that decision. You will be far from disappointed and you will soon find that it is one of the best decisions and commitments you have ever made.

STUDENT LOANS

For most people, hearing the words **"Student Loans"** brings on a gut wrenching feeling of discomfort. "Student loans" would more aptly be named "student groans" because for most, taking out a student loan is more of a curse than a blessing. We are taught at a very young age that school is critically important and that having an education is one of the best things you can obtain in life. I definitely believe that this is true: knowledge, of course, is power and school is one of the best places to obtain knowledge.

There exists, however, a major problem in regards to the education system: knowledge is expensive! A fair price tag for a college education is around $35,000. Think about it...that price is considered to be fair and many students wish they were lucky enough to go to a school that "cheap." The cost of college can range anywhere from $20,000 to over $100,000 per year. College costs can exceed the amount of money some people make in a year; and many people do not have $20k to $100k readily available in order to pay for school.

Wait! There is hope. If you don't have the money to pay for school, all is not lost. You can take out a student loan! Now, I will admit that student loans do have their perks when compared to other loans: lower interest rates and an extended period of time in which you do not have to make payments on the loans, are two such perks. However, unlike any other loan, a student loan is something that will definitely have to be paid back, even if you are unable to work, are injured, or even die! The responsibility would then just fall on your family. This is because most student loans are backed by the government and there are laws in place that prevent you from not paying back your student loans.

So here you are, fresh out of high school and full of hopes, dreams, and determination; and the first thing the government does is to put you in debt and therefore, in their power. You have just started the race yet you are already lagging behind. This is why I believe the education system is flawed. Not only do they not teach you how to use, handle, and manage your credit, they do the exact opposite and throw you into debt.

Here is a piece of advice that, while it may be controversial, I find to be true nonetheless. When choosing to go to college and pursue a degree, choose a degree that is going to make money. Now, I know many people will say that life is not all about money and that you should do what you love. I agree with this. However, if you are going to take out thousands of dollars in student loans to pursue a degree that will not make money, you are wasting your time and might as well be burning your money. I say this because it is true. You can go to school and train to become a doctor and you may even take out hundreds of thousands of dollars in loans. However, that is an occupation that is literally almost guaranteed to be worth the money and you will be able to pay back those loans. If you decide to pursue a degree that is not hot in the job market, you will struggle to pay back your loans. It is a harsh reality. Even doctors spend years paying back their loans and it can be quite the headache despite their occupation being one of the better paying jobs in America.

Student loans can easily become a catalyst for disaster and it is a way for the government to get into your pockets and to stay there. There are better and smarter options out there and for those of you who must go to college and must take out a loan, I will try to help you understand your options.

To begin, for you parents of kids, and you students, who are not yet in college or ready to go to college, I have some advice I hope you can employ. Realize that high school grades are critically important. These grades can be the difference between spending tens of thousands of dollars a year on college and spending only a few thousand dollars at most. There are numerous universities and colleges out there that offer scholarships and grants to help pay for school. A lot of these scholarships and grants are **Need-based** and dependent upon your financial success. There are also a lot of schools that offer **Merit based Scholarships**. This is basically the school giving you money and paying you to go to their school. All you have to do is get good grades and test scores. I understand that this is not easy and not possible for all, but the point is that a little extra hard work can go a long way in the long run.

Now, scholarships given by the school are not the only scholarships you can receive. If you simply open your web browser or Google and type in "scholarships" you will be able to find thousands of scholarships that you can apply for. These scholarships are usually given to students by companies, organizations, etc. For a majority of these scholarships, the most you have to do is submit some paperwork (transcripts, application, an essay, etc.). You can even search for scholarships based on your qualifications. Are you short? Tall? A minority? Do you want to major in science or math? Are you interested in the army? Do you love to play sports? Sing? Dance? No matter who you are, what you are, or what you like to do, there is no doubt a scholarship out there that you can apply for in order to take the edge off your college costs. You just have to be willing to do some extra work.

Let's say you have a scholarship but it doesn't cover all of the costs, or you just don't want to apply for any scholar-

THE POWER OF CREDIT IS IN YOUR HANDS

ships or were unable to get any. The student loan, albeit not the best, is still an option. There are two main types of student loans offered by the government and given directly to students. These are **Federal Direct loans** and may either be **subsidized** or **unsubsidized**. If you have no choice but to take out a loan, then a subsidized loan will be your friend if you can qualify for it and if your university decides to offer it to you. A subsidized loan is your friend for one simple reason: you do not have to pay interest or make any payments until six months after you graduate from college. Any interest that the loan accrues will be paid for by the government, meaning you only have to pay off the principle after you graduate. On the other hand is the unsubsidized loan. In some cases you may not qualify for a subsidized loan; perhaps you make "too much money" in the eyes of your university, or perhaps your university only offers unsubsidized loans. Either way, I don't too much like unsubsidized loans. Unsubsidized loans accrue interest and this interest is not paid by the government. You must make payments on both the interest and the principle otherwise, depending on how much you take out, your loan could multiply exponentially by time you graduate. There is a daily interest formula given on the official website for government student loans that will help you calculate how much interest accrues on your loan from month to month. It is as follows:

Outstanding Principle Balance

X Number of Days since Last Payment

X the interest rate factor (interest rate divided by number

of days in the year)

There are other types of loans available depending on who you are and what you're looking for. **A PLUS loan** is a loan that a parent can take out for their child's education. However, these loans tend to have higher interest rates and also accrue interest that is not paid by the government. **A Perkins loan** is available only to those who qualify as being in critical financial need. A middle-class or above family would most likely not qualify for a Perkins loan.

After you have taken out a loan, there are payment options available that will determine when and how you will repay your loan. The first one we will discuss is called **Deferment**. This plan is similar to a subsidized loan in that you do not have to make any payments until after you graduate. However, even if you have the deferment payment plan set up, if you have an unsubsidized loan, interest will still accumulate monthly and if left unpaid, will capitalize, or be added, to your principle. So, basically, the deferment plan allows you to wait until after graduation to begin making payments and is useful if you have an unsubsidized loan or if you cannot pay off your subsidized loan within the 6 month allotted time frame. Take note that the deferment plan only last three years. The next payment plan you may utilize is called **Forbearance**. Forbearance is similar to deferment. With forbearance you can request to stop making payments or to reduce your payments for up to 12 months. However Interest will still continue to accrue on your loans. There are eligibility requirements for both deferment and forbearance and you must contact your lender in order to request one of these payment options. You may be eligible if you:

- Are enrolled at least half-time in school
- Have an illness or injury that prevents you from working
- Are in the military
- Are studying in a fellowship or graduate school
- Are experiencing economic hardship

You must continue to make all payments on your loans until you have been approved for either payment plan. If you stop making payments, serious consequences can ensue and you will be labeled as **delinquent and default** on your loan; defaulting would then cause serious legal consequences.

The next two options you have are **loan consolidation** and **rehabilitation**. Consolidating your loans simply means that you will group together all the loans you have taken out and lump them into one big loan. This allows for easier payments; you don't have to worry about paying Loan A on the 20th then Loan B on the 30th and so on. The downside is that it can end up taking longer to pay off the consolidated loan because your payments may be smaller than the individual payments you would have been making. Rehabilitation is exactly what it sounds like: you're going to student loan rehab. If you haven't made payments in a long time or have defaulted on your loan it is possible to get the loan reinstated and to get the negative items off your credit report. Contact your lender to see if you are eligible for the program and get an agreement in writing. After making a few initial payments – 9 in about 10 months – the loan will be reinstated and will be placed in good standing and the negative markings on your report will be removed. This option also stops **wage garnishments and income tax withholdings.**

Always remember that there are options for student loan repayments. Contact your lender, explain your situation, discuss your options, and ask for a payment plan. Do not just stop paying. Your credit will suffer and legal action can be taken against you and we do not want that. Student loans can be either a blessing or a curse but honestly, it all depends on you.

NOW TELL ME WHAT TO DO: The Do's and Don'ts of Managing Your Credit

The first few chapters stressed the critical importance of having good credit. But now that you know how important credit is, I am sure that you have some questions and concerns. One of the most common things that I hear from people I meet and help is:

Tell me what to do. That is actually a very powerful statement: "Tell me what to do." For one, it means that people have started to take the first steps towards improving not only their credit, but their lives as well. It also means that people trust me to help them.

Although I cannot dictate anyone's life, I can offer my knowledge and advice. There are a few tips that I am going to give you to start off with. I mentioned some of these tips in the previous chapters but I will reiterate and expound upon them now. Once you have these tips down pact, you will definitely notice a positive change in your credit score and will improve your financial wellbeing.

DO: Always, always *pay on time*.
Considering that your payment history is the biggest percentage when it comes to calculating your credit score, it is crucial that you make all payments punctually. Here is another gem I want you to have and remember. If possible, make credit card payments before the reporting date (more on this piece of advice later). It is very important to also keep in mind that your newest credit is among your most important credit. Regardless of what your past credit habits were or what you did or didn't do with your credit, it is important that from today onwards you start developing good credit habits. Make it your top priority to make timely payments.

DON'T: *Be late or miss a payment*;
once again, payment history is one of the biggest components used when calculating your FICO Score. Making late payments can lead to serious consequences. You can be charged a late fee, your interest rates may rise, the late payment marking will be reflected on your credit report, and your credit score may sink. It is a good idea to gather all of your loans and bills and to write down when all of their

payments are due and their reporting date. Do whatever you can to make sure that all of your bills are paid on time. Try not to let more than 30 days elapse before making your payments otherwise it is highly possible that it will show up on your credit report as a negative mark.

DO: Watch your *usage of available credit*.
As stated before, you want to keep your utilization at or below 30%. Remember that utilization plays a big role in your credit scoring. If you have credit cards that are maxed out, your credit score will suffer. Do whatever you can to get any credit cards you own to a balance below 30%. I cannot stress this enough. To put this in perspective, imagine that you loan someone $1,000 and tell them to use it as they see fit. All they have to do is pay you back on the first of the month. The first of the month arrives and you check to see how much of the $1,000 has been used.
How would you feel if the entire amount had been used? Your first thought might be along the lines of, "Is this person going to be able to pay me back?" Your next thought might be, "Well what exactly was the money used for?"
On the other hand, if you saw that only $300 of the $1,000 had been used, you would feel more comfortable. Or imagine, if you gave a child $20 to go to the candy store and they only used $3, not only would you feel good, but you would feel more inclined to give that child more money in the future. You can trust them to use your money responsibly. This is how lenders view credit so it is important

that you don't abuse the credit given to you.

DON'T: Max out any of your credit cards.

If you have a few credit cards but one of them is your absolute favorite, try to spread out the usage. If one credit card is maxed out, don't be afraid to transfer balances so that you can meet the 30% mark. Also make sure that the credit card or cards with the higher limits get paid off first. Let's show the CRAs that we know how to responsibly manage our credit and keep those balances down.

DO: *Age your accounts.*

What does that mean? Simply, the older your accounts, the better. Recall that Length of History was a component of your credit scoring. Aging your accounts will help to improve your credit file and credit score. Since older accounts are preferable, if you have too many open accounts, try to close the newer ones. If your older accounts are always paid off and there is no bad history regarding them, this will look good to lenders. It exemplifies to them and CRAs that you can be trusted both short and long term. Also try to open up accounts early on in life and let them age. Be sure to remember this piece of advice because I am going to reveal a big secret later in this book that I guarantee will change how you play the game of credit.

DON'T: *Close older accounts.*

I have seen many people make the mistake of closing older accounts because they do not use them anymore. It is far from a good idea to do this. Also try to avoid opening too many new accounts; this brings the age average down. So, that old credit card account from freshmen year of college? Keep it. This will only help to make your credit file stronger.

This next piece of advice goes hand in hand with the aforementioned tip.

DO: Make sure to *minimize new credit.*
You don't want to open up too many new accounts too fast. Doing so would affect the aging of your accounts as mentioned before. Also, lenders and CRAs would view too many new accounts as a negative thing. Imagine opening up three new accounts for $3,000 each and then maxing all of them out. That would paint a picture of you being irresponsible and lenders would doubt your ability to repay all of that debt. When structuring your credit, it is essential that you keep in mind how the lenders will perceive you. They are, after all, the people who will decide whether or not to approve you for a loan; therefore, it is best to give them a picture perfect profile. This applies to how the CRAs and their FICO Score processing software will view you as well.

DON'T: *Make too many inquiries.*
An inquiry is simply whenever you, or someone else, requests your credit file. There are two types of inquiries: **a hard pull and a soft pull.** A soft pull inquiry does not have the same potential for credit disaster as a hard pull possesses. A hard pull occurs when you request your credit file to apply for credit (credit cards, car, house etc.) A soft pull

occurs when companies request your file in order to make you credit card offers and such. So why are too many inquiries a bad thing? Well when your credit file is pulled for an inquiry too many times, it paints a picture of irresponsibility and "thirstiness." Imagine that you are seeking a new car; at every dealership you visit, your credit file will be pulled. If your search for a car lasts no more than a week or two and your file is pulled a number of times, this will not harm your credit score. That week or two is considered a grace period so that you can shop around for the best interest rates. However, if you continuously have inquiries made into your credit file over a longer period (say, a month or two), this will make you seem as if you are being irresponsible with how you handle your credit.

Why is this person visiting so many car dealerships?
How many cars is this person trying to buy?
Can this person be trusted to make payments on so many vehicles?

Even if you are not actually going to purchase an army of vehicles, having so many inquiries into your credit will certainly raise those questions within CRAs and lenders. They, in turn, will not assume very highly of you. Also note that every time you pull your credit report to apply for credit, your score loses some points. Let's say you go out and apply for three credit cards and for each inquiry, you lose let's say 5 points. Well now your credit score has just been knocked down by 15 points. In such a case as this, it is better to wait a period of time between opening multiple credit cards for there is no grace period for opening credit card accounts.

DO: Mix up your accounts and *add variety.*
If you were to submit a résumé to an employer, the more work experience and variety you presented, the more likely you are to be hired. By adding variety to your file, you are showing that you know how to manage your credit in more than one way. You can add variety to your account by having **1-3 revolving accounts (i.e. credit cards) and an installment loan such as a car or mortgage.** This variety exemplifies that you can take care of the small matters (credit cards) and the big ones (car, mortgage, etc.). Doing this will definitely improve your credit profile.
These are just a few simple but very effective tips that will help you get started on the path to better credit and finances.

DO: *Heed these simple rules.*
I guarantee you will notice a positive change in your financial life. There is, after all, a system in place that calculates your credit score. To maximize the amount of points your score can receive, you have to play by the rules of the system. Learn to play its game and you'll be the real MVP in no time.

TOO LATE.
Now What?

0%   10%   25%

The previous chapters touched on some very useful tips that will help to strengthen and build your credit and prevent it from going bad. However for some people it is just too late and their credit is basically down the drain. This chapter is for those people.

There have been plenty of times I've caught myself thinking, "If only I knew then, what I know now." Unfortunately, hindsight is always 20/20. If your credit is at a point where you feel like there is no hope and that it will never get to where it needs to be, do not fret; there is hope. No matter the reason for your bad credit (divorce, unemployment, injuries, lack of knowledge, etc.) your credit can be saved. Luckily for you, you picked up this book and are now in this chapter. Reading this chapter will help you to get your credit back on track and on its way to being respectable. Many people think this process is hopeless or will take forever but that is not the case. In reality you can improve your credit and see positive changes in as little as 30 to 45 days.

The first thing that I suggest to do is to get an up to date copy of your credit report from all three bureaus. Once you have that, you can see what and where the actual damage is according to all three reports. Now that you know how to read your credit report, doing this will be easy and you will know what you are looking for and where to find it.

Before we go any further, I want you to grab a pen and a paper because we are going to start taking some notes. If you are 100% committed to fixing your credit, this process is going to be fairly quick and easy.

Alright, here is what you need to do: look at your credit report and write down every negative item listed. On a separate sheet of paper, write down all of the positive items. Then try to break down the negative items into categories: those that are marked 30 days late, 60 days late, 90 days late, and 150 days late but are not labeled as a charge off. For the items that are 30 days late, write the word **"Goodwill"** next to them. For the items marked 60 days late, write the word "goodwill" or **"FCBA"** next to them. Then for the items that are 90-150 days late, write the word "FCBA" next to them. FCBA stands for **Fair Credit Billing Act**. We will come back to these items later.

You may come across some negative items labeled

as a **Collection Unpaid** from a Collection Agency. Next to these items, write the word **"Validation"**. You then may come across some negative items labeled as a **Collection Unpaid by the Original Creditor**. Next to these, write the word **"Investigation."** The next items you may encounter will be marked **Paid Collection.** Next to these, also write the word **"Investigation."** Finally, you may see some items marked with the words **"Charge Off."** Next to these items, write the word **"Investigation."**

On the items marked 30-60 days late, you can write what is called a Goodwill Letter. This is basically a letter where you ask for forgiveness for being late and explain that you are now up to date with your payments. You then go on to ask if it is possible for a favor to be granted and if the negative items can be removed from your credit report. Be sure to write the letter in your own words, give valid and good reasons as to why you were late (funeral, out of town, moved, etc.). Give the reason why you are writing the letter (buying a house or car, trying to better your life, etc.), and make sure to sound sincere. Do not be pushy in the letter and be sure to exemplify that you are taking responsibility for your mistakes. Remind them that you are a good customer and despite your mistakes, you will remain a good costumer. In a nutshell, the letter is basically saying "hey I messed up and made a mistake. I won't do it again. Please forgive me and remove the late pays." This is a pretty effective way to deal with those negative marks. Although it is not guaranteed that they will be removed, it is better to try because the chances are still pretty good that it will work. However, do not worry if this step doesn't work; we have other options at our disposal that we will discuss later in the book. You can find Goodwill sample letters in the back of the book.

Next on our list are the items that are **90-150 days late but are not charged off.** With these items, we are going to take a different approach and use one of our many rights that we possess through congress, which gives us in order to protect us when it comes to our credit. This right is called the **FCBA.** With this Act, the creditors are required to provide certain documentation and information regarding your account. If they cannot provide the documentation, that you requested through the FCBA. Then you can notify the CRAs and ask them to remove the items. With these items, you do not need to provide any reasons. You can just exercise your rights.

Keep in mind that as we work to improve your credit, any items listed on your credit report must be verified. This is something that a lot of people don't know. The CRAs do not verify any information given to them unless you request that information to be verified. This is one of the biggest keys to this whole process and one of the biggest problems in the credit reporting system.

The next items on our list are those labeled **Collections.** For the unpaid collections, you are going to exercise **the FCRA. Fair Credit Reporting Act.** This means that the CRAs will have to investigate and verify those items. They have a 30 day window to do so and if the collection agency cannot provide the proper documentation to the CRAs, by law the negative items will have to be removed from your credit report. For the items marked Collection Unpaid by the Original Creditor and Collections labeled Paid Charge offs, you are also going to use the FCRA as well. Just the same as the Goodwill Letter, the investigation technique is not guaranteed to work but the chances are still pretty good. The reason for this is because most Collection Agencies don't provide the proper information to the CRAs in time permitted.

There are sample dispute letters in the back of the book. Use them as a reference for formatting but remember to use your own words and to be genuine. Also make sure to send all of the letters by Certified Mail so that you can know for sure when the clock starts ticking, so to speak. These are just a few strategies you can use to try to get those negative items off your report. After you receive the results of the investigations and Goodwill Letters, your credit score will improve from the negative items removed, and for any items that were not removed, you can dispute these items again if you believe they do not belong there. For those items that are still there but do belong, there is a way to fix them and I will discuss those solutions later. I will also show you how you can settle the amount owed for a much lower amount and then try to get it removed.
Now that some of the negative items have been removed, we will start adding positive items.

You can begin by implementing the advice given in the chapters **"The Do's and Don'ts of Credit and Credit from the Ground Up."** Doing so will improve your credit rating, your credit report, and your credit habits.

CREDIT:
The Secret to Success

Now that we have covered quite a bit of information and we have a better understanding of credit, let's discuss in detail why credit is so crucial. When I first began to do research on credit there was a word that kept popping up; that word is **"Secret."** I label credit as the things to many things: World's best kept secret, the Secret they don't want you to know, etc. The one that stood out the most to me was **"The secret to success."** Credit is so important and valuable in today's society. When making major purchases in life, such as a car or a home, it is guaranteed that you will need to have at least an average credit score in order to qualify for such loans. Even if you do qualify with subpar credit, the interest rates will be abominably high.

The value of credit is highly underestimated and it is done so on purpose. If everyone knew the true value of credit and how to make it work for them, there would be an overflow of successful people and perhaps even more millionaires. The business of lending is one of the biggest industries on earth due to the trillions of dollars being exchanged at varying interest rates. The lower your credit score, the higher the interest rate; the higher the interest rates, the more you pay and the more they make. Saving 1% on an interest rate can be the difference in tens of thousands of dollars. It is clear to see that credit is important and valuable. But let's discuss how it can make you successful.

Making powerful investments in life, such as real estate or opening up a business can take tons of money and it can take more money than most people have available. This is where the value of credit comes in. With a good credit score, making investments without having the cash is extremely possible. When you build your credit file exactly the way it's supposed to be, it makes it so much easier for lenders to decide to loan you money no matter what type of purchase or investment you wish to make.

I want you to ask yourself a question you may never have heard before. It is an important question and I want you to think about it before you answer: What is your John Hancock worth? I stumbled across that question one day and it truly stuck with me and resonated within me. I know some people who can sign their name on a piece of paper and drive off a car lot with a half a million dollar car. I also know some people, like my uncle who would say "If I sign there it would just be a waste of ink." I know some real estate investors who would purchase income generating properties with just a signature on a few pages of paperwork. I know even more people who wouldn't be able to rent a trunk to live in if their life depended on it. You see, there is power in the pen and it takes discipline and dedication to reach the level where you can just sign your name and make your dreams come true.

When it comes to opening a business, banks are willing to give small business startup loans to get a business off the ground, but it all depends on your credit score. They want someone who is guaranteed to repay the money, a **Personal Guarantor.**

So no matter what you are doing: making a big purchase, starting up a new business, or being a real estate mogul, your credit will always be a major decision factor. This is the reason why credit is the secret to success and taking care of your credit can truly lead to the American Dream or at least financial stability. Many of the world's richest people were not born with money but made their fortune through knowledge and innovation and of course, good credit.

A very wise person once told me to build my success by using other people's money, OPM. Use the banks money and credit to fund your dreams, accomplish your goals, and build a better life. Just be sure to use it wisely and following the advice in the previous chapters can definitely help with that. Credit is the Secret to Success and now you know that secret. Don't hush, tell everyone.

CORPORATE CREDIT

In this chapter I want to go over the importance of establishing and the building of corporate credit. For those of you who already have an established corporation we will discuss what you can do to get started. For those who are looking to start a business this chapter will cover some of the basics. **Corporate Credit first and foremost is not the same as your personal credit.** Though the two will have a lot to do with each other they are completely different.

The first step in establishing business credit is to create a **Corporation** or a **Limited liability corporation also known as a LLC.** Once you have done that you will want to apply for a **Tax ID number**. Getting this number separates the business from your personal social security number and allows the business to become its own entity. Then you want to make sure you acquire a business address and phone number one that is different from your own home address and personal number. Doing this makes the business look legitimate and remember with lenders it's all about how they perceive you.

Once you have the Corporation or LLC, the tax id, address and phone number you can then go to your bank and **open up a Business account**. Most banks have programs and benefits they offer for Business accounts. It is always good to explore your options and always keep your business accounts separate from your personal accounts. It is always good to build a business relationship with your banker. Sit down with him or her and go over your plan. When opening a business it is always good to make sure you have a business plan. There is a saying that I truly believe and it's **"If you fail to plan it is because you plan to fail."**

Now what you want to do is contact one of the credit reporting agencies that reports corporate credit. One of the more known Agencies that you can contact is **Dun and Bradstreet or also known as D&B.** When you contact them tell them you want to register your business with them and request your **Data Universal Numbering System or better known as your DUNS number.** The DUNS number uses a system much like the one used with your personal credit to calculate what is known as a Paydex Score. Now remember you have a FICO score which is your personal credit score and now a **Paydex score** which is your business credit score. The Paydex score point system is setup much different from that of the FICO score point system but with some of the same techniques and principles. The **Paydex score ranges from 1 to 100.** You want your Paydex rating to be 80 or above. Now that you are registered with D&B and have your DUNS Number it is time to start building your Corporate Credit. You want to start small by applying for office supply cards such as Stables, Office Max, etc. These cards are a little easier to get. You want to apply for one or two and then space out the time for applying for more at least a month or so. Most lenders and retailers want to see that your business has been open for at least two years before approving any credit. Some lenders will even go to the extent of asking for the company cash flow records and a business plan outlining exactly how the credit will be used. They might ask to see any licenses or certifications needed to operate the business, insurance policies, and bank statements.

Once you have been approved for these smaller credit card limits like $300 and $500. What you want to do is use $50 to $100 on each card and then make sure just like with your personal credit that you pay the bill on or before the due date. Keep in mind that with any credit card or loan you have to always find out the bill due date and the reporting date. When applying for these credit cards it is very important to make sure these cards report to the credit reporting agencies otherwise you will not get the results you are looking for and will be wasting your time. After getting, using and paying on these office supply cards for a few months and have built up some Paydex points. It will be time to apply for some gas cards. Typically these cards are a little harder to get and may even require a **Personal Guarantor.**

A personal guarantor is when you put your personal credit on the contract to guarantee the company that the debt or loan will be paid back. After getting the office supply cards and now the gas cards and using them, wait another few months. At this point you can now attempt to get some of the bigger commercial credit cards such as Home Depot, Lowes, Menards, etc. After you have established and built your Paydex score you will now go to your banker who you went over your business plan with and apply for a small loan. After borrowing and paying back some these smaller loans you will be able to qualify for some bigger loans. Some of the better business credit cards to get as far as lines of credit goes are from Bank of America, Capital One, Citi Group, and American Express. Each bank has its own specific cards and programs they offer so again do your research and weigh your options. These steps should help you in reaching your business goals.

I know things don't always go according to plan. For instance if you're a new business and don't have the two year history of being established most lenders and vendors are looking for, you can run into some stumbling blocks. If this is the case don't worry you still have options. You can open up a **Secured Business Card**. There are no two year requirements, proof of cash flow, DTI which is debt to income, bank statements etc. The way the lenders look at it is they have collateral in exchange for the business credit card. It limits their risk in approving your company for the credit limit.

Now as you know from reading the book I like to pass down what I like to call Gems or Secrets to the Trade. I am going to give you another one now to help you reach your goal of building corporate credit. Most of the Retailers that report to the Credit reporting agencies don't report to them right of way. Most of them are back logged three to six months if not more. So it will take them that long to report your activity with their company to the CRA. A way to get the results you are looking for faster is to purchase products directly from D&B. They are linked with a lot of the same companies you will be dealing with. Purchasing directly from D&B allows that transaction to report automatically and will raise your Paydex score much quicker. See their system reports the activity automatically. Keep this in mind as you are striving to reach your business goals.

I strongly recommend all business owners establish and build their corporate credit rating. Though business might be good now, you never know what could happen in the future. Having good corporate credit may be the difference between the business surviving a hardship or having to close the doors permanently. Good luck in your business adventures and may all your goals be reached.

MORTGAGE READY

When it comes to credit and the many benefits of having good credit there is one benefit that stands out to me above the rest. That benefit is purchasing a home. The luxury of being able to buy a house and not have to pay all the money for that house up front is by far the best thing about having good credit. Think about it for a minute. What if this option wasn't available? If in order to purchase a home you had to pay for it in full, upfront. How many people do you think would actually be able to ever own a home? Not many that is for sure. The purchase of a home is most likely the biggest debt that will ever go on your credit. The average sales price in the Chicagoland area in 2013 was around $170,000.00.

Purchasing a house or a property is a huge accomplishment but an even bigger responsibility. It can be become a dream come true. However as I have said before the American Dream can quickly become the American Nightmare. Let's just be wise and informed before making such a big move in life and everything can turn out great. Before you can get to the point of owning your own home or property. Your credit file has to be structured properly so that a bank or lender will qualify you for a loan for such a big purchase. I will go over some of the requirements so that you can get approved for such a loan.

Most lenders are looking for a minimum middle score of 620. As you know there are three credit bureaus and each one gives you a score. The middle score is just that the one in the middle. If on TransUnion your score is 650, on Equifax it is a 610 and on Experian it is a 630. Your middle is a 630. Eliminate your highest and lowest score and the one that's left is your middle score. Now even though your middle score is 630 and higher than the 620 requirement, it is possible that you still may not qualify for the loan. As we discussed in previous chapters the lenders want to see more than just a 620 middle score. They want to see at least three trade lines. **A trade line is a credit card, car loan, installment loan etc. Anytime you finance something and it is being reported on your credit that can be considered a trade line.** So again the lenders want to see at least three trade lines. Those trade lines have to be at least 12 months old. (The qualifications vary from state to state and lender to lender). The reason they want to see the three trade lines is so they know you have established credit more than once before allowing you to borrow such a large amount.

Structuring your credit file with a variety and also having a good length of history will definitely work in your favor when it comes time to buy a home. The credit file is just one aspect of the qualification process. The lenders will want to know that if they loan you let's say $200,000.00 for a property that you are going to be able to make the monthly mortgage payments. Therefore another part of getting approved will be your income. They are going to want to see your two most recent years of income tax returns. How much you make will determine how much you can borrow. When it comes to getting such a large loan the lenders are going to look at every inch of your financial existence. With credit there is a term that lending institutions use and that is **Debt To Income Ratio**. **D.T.I.R.** is simply put as how much money do you make and how much of that money goes to paying off debt. Another term is Debt to credit ratio. This is basically how much total credit you have and how much of that credit has been used. They look at both of these to determine how much you can qualify for.

What they do is subtract how much you have to pay out from how much you make to determine how much you can afford. It is important that you don't take out too many loans or max out your credit cards if you are considering buying a home unless you have a big enough income to show you can afford it. The lenders don't usually want to finance a loan for a property to a person that has a debt to income ratio greater than 42%. Which means if 42% or more of your total income is going to pay off debt than chances are you won't get approved for the loan. So far we know we have to have a credit score of 620 or higher with three or more trade lines that are at least 12 months old and two years of income tax returns and W2s showing how much you make.

The next on the list of things needed are your check stubs. They are going to want to see your two most recent pay stubs. Then they are going to ask for your two most recent bank statements. It is great if you have your pay check set up for direct deposit to show the banks that the money that will be used to pay back the loan goes in your account automatically. With your bank statements it is important to not have any over drafts or bounced checks within the two month period prior to applying for the loan as this can draw a red flag and affect your chances of getting approved. It is also good to show that you are saving money as well as you will need it for a down payment.

Through an FHA loan which is a government backed loan, the minimum down payment requirement is 3.5% of the purchase price of the property. Which means $3,500.00 for every $100,000.00. So on a $200,000.00 loan the down payment would be $7,000.00. There are other fees that are applied that you can talk to your mortgage broker or realtor about such as closing cost, title fees etc.

One of the benefits of going through FHA is they allow the down payment to be a gift from a close family member (mother, father, brother, sister). So now you have a general idea of the five major requirements needed in getting approved for a home loan and being Mortgage Ready.

1. **Credit score of 620 or higher.**
2. **Two most recent years of income taxes.**
3. **Two most recent pay stubs.**
4. **Three most recent bank statements.**
5. **Down payment at least 3.5%.**

Here is a list of other documentation that might be asked of you by the lender. Two year resident history

Social security card

VA certification or eligibility

DD214 (For Military)

Monthly debt information

Child support/child care

Divorce decree

Lease agreement/ rent receipts

Mortgage and account numbers

Driver's license or state I.D.

These are just a few things that might be asked for and again it varies state to state lender to lender. Remember purchasing a home can be a dream come true and it is a huge commitment. Make sure you are financially disciplined and able before doing so.

I have seen so many people live long happy times in their homes and unfortunately I have seen many people lose their homes to foreclosure and completely ruin their credit and lives. There are a lot of great programs available that can help you with down payment and closing cost, so be sure to do your research before buying your home. I hope this information helps and makes the sometimes very stressful process of purchasing a property a little easier to understand. Good luck and may all your dreams and wishes come true.

DEALING WITH DEBT

In this day and age being debt free is almost unheard of. There are a multitude of ways someone can incur debt: student loans, credit cards, car loans, mortgages, etc. The list goes on and on. The point is that a lot of people are in debt and are suffering because of it. Debt can literally be a killer: it can kill your joy, your energy, your marriage, etc. Debt is in every sense of the word bad. The average American family owes anywhere from 30k to 50k in credit card debt. And instead of helping people get out of debt, banks and creditors purposely make it harder by hiking up interest rates when you miss payments.

Fortunately you have picked up this book and I am here to tell you that there is hope; debt cannot kill that. This chapter is designed to inform you about how you can get out of debt by discussing how to **Negotiate,**

Settle, and Eliminate your debt. I'm not going to waste time telling you how to lower your payments, interest rates, etc. I want your debt to be **nonexistent.** And I am going to try to help you do this by paying **50%** or less of what you initially owed.

Debt settlement is an aggressive approach and it is not for everyone. I certainly recommend that you avoid going through a third party for debt settlement. You will only end up owing an arm, a leg, and your firstborn to the third party. The **DIY (do it yourself)** approach is better and not to mention cheaper; you can get the same results and save a lot of money in the process.

There are five basic strategies to use when you are dealing with bad debt:

1.   **Debt Roll-Up** – This strategy is simple to understand. You simply pay more than the minimum payment. If your minimum payment is $200, send in a payment of $300. Always be sure to pay at least the minimum on your debt. Prioritizing your debt from the smallest to the largest will be a useful strategy. Paying off the smaller debts first will be a wise thing to do because it will eliminate that debt and free up money as you move forward to paying the bigger debts. This strategy is for those individuals who are good at keeping track of their debt.

2.   **Debt Consolidation** – This method is similar to consolidating a loan. Let's say you owe $1,000 to three different lenders. You cannot afford to pay a total of $300 a month to each lender. So you consolidate your debt. Now instead of paying $900, you write a check for $350 and the money is split between the three lenders. This is a monthly payment until what you owe eventually reaches $0. I warn you, however, to beware of scam artists. Scam companies will say "We will work out settlements with your lenders if you give us $450 to give to them." In reality what will happen is this: you will pay the $450 to the scam company and then never hear from them again and you will still be in debt. Scam companies will prey upon your desperation so be vigilant.

3.   **Borrow the Money** – Consider borrowing money from a finance company to pay off your debts. Sounds a bit silly to borrow money to pay back borrowed money but this can actually be beneficial. Let's say you owe $20,000 to a lender with a 17% interest rate. It would be cheaper for you to borrow that money from a finance company at let's say, a 7% interest rate and to use that money to pay off the debt with the higher interest rate. You will still owe $20,000 but now it would be at a much lower interest rate than before. The difficult part is securing the loan without having to put up collateral and this is overall a difficult technique but it is still a viable option.

4.   **Equity** – This option is based upon your ownership of real estate. **Equity is the difference between what you owe on your home versus what it is worth.** If you owe less than what your home is worth then you have equity. If you owe more than what your home is worth then you are considered to be **"underwater" or "upside down"** and therefore have no equity. This technique is only recommended for the highly disciplined. If you have $20,000 worth of equity and find a lender that allows you to take that equity out, you can use it to pay off your credit card debt. However, this can be a bad idea for those who aren't as disciplined. Now you have paid off your credit card debt and you now have full usage of the credit card again. If you are not disciplined and you max out the card again, you will then be in debt again and out of $20,000 of equity. You also have exchanged an **unsecure debt (credit card)** for a **secured debt (mortgage)** which now means you have more to lose than a good credit rating. Therefore if this technique isn't used with great care, it can be more harmful than beneficial.

5.   **Credit Counseling** – This option is one that generally receives negative reviews but I will list it anyway because it can help. If you seek out a credit counselor what mostly happens is that you are enrolled in a program where you pay a monthly fee to the credit counselor and they will then disburse that money to the

different creditors you owe. Only downside is that you are paying the credit counselor to do this when you can probably do it yourself. Most people drop out of the program for lack of quick results. However, if you employ the help of a credit counselor who is genuine in his or her desire to help you, your results will be very positive.

6.   **Bankruptcy** – This is a last ditch effort for those of you who are absolutely drowning in debt with no way out. When you declare bankruptcy it forces all commercial creditors from harassing and trying to collect from you. Wage garnishments, reverses, and judgments will be stopped and most of your debt can be wiped out, depending on what type of bankruptcy you file. There is a strong misconception about bankruptcy and most view it as credit suicide but this is far from the truth. There are two types of bankruptcy, chapter 7 and chapter 13. Chapter 7 is the preferred choice but is difficult to file due to stricter laws. Chapter 13 is less preferred because you will end up having to pay off most of your debt within a five year period and the bankruptcy will appear on your report for the next ten years. Chapter 7 is slightly more preferred because some of your property is protected from collection by the creditors but the blemish will still appear on your report for the next ten years. I recommend seeking counseling before choosing this path and exploring every other option available. Although bankruptcy is not credit suicide, it is really close.

7.   **Debt Settlement** – This is one of the best ways to handle debt in my opinion. Debt settlement can lead to your debt being cut nearly in half if not more. Creditors would rather close an account at 50% than not get anything at all. Basically you have to show the creditors what you have, let them know that it is all you have, and they can either take it or leave it. Most of the time they will take it. If you choose to go this route be sure to **get everything in writing** and to already have your money available. You will be able to see your debt vanish in no time.

These techniques will be useful in helping you deal with your debt but it is up to you to commit to employing these techniques the right way. Don't spend the rest of your life ignoring your debt, screening phone calls, and living in constant worry. Being debt free creates a peace of mind that I can only describe as being happy. Therefore I urge you to explore your options, start with the ones listed here and then delve deeper if necessary. At the end of the day, owing nothing to anyone will be one of the best feelings you will ever feel.

PROMISES

In my life I have experienced long periods of time when I was in debt. I struggled and lived from paycheck to paycheck and sometimes there just was no paycheck or any source of income at all. I borrowed, begged, and sometimes just went without certain things.

In the process I learned many valuable lessons: **never give up and never put myself in that situation again.** I forced myself to practice better spending habits, better saving habits, and more importantly, better paying habits. I would rather have no money in my bank account and my bills paid than to have pockets full of money and lingering debt.

I had hardships thanks to my debt and at one

point I honestly tried to get out of debt by seeking the aid of professionals. I ended up getting scammed by a company who promised a perfect credit rating in 30 days or less. Desperate yet full of hope to have my credit repaired, I paid the outrageous fee the company charged and waited to have my dream of perfect credit come true. Unfortunately, after waiting several months, I never heard from the company again. That was the last straw. I did not want to depend on anyone else. I wanted to learn how to help myself, and I did. Now I truly desire to help you because I know how it feels to struggle and have your hopes crushed by false promises.

Don't fall for scams. If someone says they can wipe your debt away or give you a perfect credit score and all you have to do is pay them, do not believe it. Fixing your credit and eliminating your debt is a process and involves steps and advice. Being scammed out of thousands of dollars is one of the reasons I decided to learn all about credit. This book is the results of that effort and I can assure you this is no scam. Simply reading the first few chapters and following the advice will reassure you of that. **Read the book, learn its content, absorb the knowledge, understand it, apply it, and then pass it on.**

IDENTITY THEFT

In this section I would like to bring to your attention one of the worst things that could happen to you and your personal credit. Identity Theft is the fastest growing crime in the United States. 1 in 6 Americans can expect to be a victim of Identity theft this year alone. With over 15 million reports filed each year it is definitely something you should be aware of and protect yourself from. The average loses on the case by case basis is approximately $3,500.00 and the total losses is in the upwards of $50 billion. Identity Theft can be devastating to your credit rating as well as your financial wellbeing. The thieves are getting smarter and with the use of technology it is becoming easier for them to steal your identity. They are hacking into major company databases and getting access to all your personal information such as bank account numbers, credit and debit card numbers, social security numbers, address, phone numbers, emails and anything else about you they might need.

With having all of this information about you assuming your identity is easier than a walk in the park. They open up new accounts, max out old accounts, wipe out bank accounts and potentially ruin people lives. This is a very serious issue.

Now that you understand the severity of Identity theft lets go over some of the ways you can protect yourself from being a victim. For those who have been or are a victim we will go over what you can do to rectify the situation and get your life back on track. In my opinion getting some sort of **Identity Theft Protection** is important to ensuring that you don't become a victim. There are many identity theft protection companies out there such as Life Lock and many others. This will make it harder for the fraudsters to steal your identity. Also making sure you shred any documents containing your personal information and even junk mail is a great idea. See there are thieves that have mastered technology and then you have the old fashion ones that go through your dumpster. Dumpster diving is a way many people have become victims of Identity Theft. They will also steal your mail so making sure you have a secured mailbox is another step you can take in protecting yourself.

Well what happens if you end up being a victim of identity theft? What do you do? Well there are steps you can take and rights that are given to victims of identity theft. Checking your credit report once a year is recommended, however I believe that you should check it no less than twice a year. With all the different credit monitoring websites that can be viewed from a smart phone there is no reason why you don't check your credit frequently. **Remember it doesn't hurt your score to monitor your credit report. It is not considered an inquiry.**

So let's say you're monitoring your report and you see something on there that doesn't belong to you or an account that you didn't open and it is being report negatively. This can and will hurt your credit rating. Fortunately you caught it after only a couple months. Now imagine if you had let a whole year go by before checking your report and seeing the fraudulent activity imagine the damage that would be done to your score. So now what you need to do is **place an initial fraud alert on your report.** How you do that is by contacting the credit reporting agencies and ask them to put a fraud alert on your file. They will do so and **this initial fraud alert will last 90 days.** The next thing to do is to order all three of your credit reports and check them for any errors or fraudulent accounts. That means to make sure that your **name, address, social security number, employers, account balances, everything is being reported accurately.** Once you have placed the initial fraud alert on your report and checked all three reports.

The next thing to do will be go to the **Federal Trade Commission** website or call them and create an **Identity Theft Report.** Now there are two parts to an Identity theft report to make it complete. First is you must submit a report about the identity theft to the FTC explaining in detail everything that happened to the best of your knowledge. Once you are done you need to print out this report. If you go to the website it will guide you on what to do. This report is called an **Identity Theft Affidavit.** Now you are going to take the identity theft affidavit with you to the police station. There you are going to file a **Police Report** about the identity theft. Once that is done be sure to get a copy of the police report. **See the identity theft affidavit and the police report together complete your identity theft report.** When you go to the police station take with you **a valid ID or Driver License and proof of address** such as a rental agreement or rent receipt and any proof of the theft you might have.

Creating an identity theft report is very important to the process of getting the issue resolved. Having this report gives you rights that will help you in dealing with the credit reporting agencies, debt collectors, and getting the fraudulent information removed from your credit report. It will stop the companies from collecting debts and or selling the debts to other companies. It will allow you to place an extended fraud alert on your report that can last 7 years. It allows you to get two free credit reports from all three companies within a twelve month period. It gets your name removed from marketing list with credit offers for five years unless you request to be put back on.

Getting the negative markings removed from your file is vital to making sure your score doesn't continue to take negative hits. If you see errors on your report like accounts you didn't open or debts you didn't incur you need to file a dispute with the credit reporting companies and the fraud department of each business reporting the inaccuracies. This is a key note: If the errors are a direct result from the identity theft and you have an identity theft report, you can ask the credit reporting companies to block the fraudulent information from appearing on your credit report. **They must block the transactions and accounts if you are a victim of identity theft.** This process isn't easy but it is worth the effort. Make sure you keep copies of all reports, request documents, and dispute letters.

Being a victim of identity theft can damage your life and credit. I hope that it never happens to you and that this information can help to prevent it from happening. If you are or have been a victim of identity theft use this information to get your credit back on track and remember that **you have rights.** Protect yourself people and remember at the end of the day it is your life were talking about. Don't wait until it's too late.

JUDGEMENT DAY

This chapter is going to discuss what happens when a judgment is brought against you. The scenario usually goes as follows: you borrowed a large sum of money, you didn't make payments, you didn't go to court and a judge ruled in favor of the creditors.

A judgment is overall just bad news. When you enter into a contract with a creditor, such as opening a credit card account, if you default on the account it will show up as a negative mark on your credit report for up to 7 years. A judgment can show up on your credit report for up to 14 years or longer. That is not the worst that can happen. Having a judgment brought against you can be worse than defaulting on a car loan. If you don't make payments on the car loan, your car will simply be repossessed. With a judgment, however, the creditors can seize more than just your car; everything will be up for grabs. Since the creditors will be paying big bucks to sue you, they will not go after you for owing a small amount and if you owe a large sum, trust that they will go after everything. Once a judgment is brought against you, any defense you might have had against the creditors will be wiped away.

There are ways you can try to avoid a judgment depending on how much you owe and whether or not the creditor believes you can pay back the money owed.

If you are sued make sure to show up to court; do not ignore the letters and court summons. This will at the very least exemplify that you care about the outcome of the lawsuit and it opens your options on what you can do to save your skin. When you go to court you can have the option of making a payment plan with the creditor or even settling the loan amount for a lower amount. If you do manage to work out a debt settlement with the creditors and their lawyers, only agree to the settlement if they agree to **drop the lawsuit.** It doesn't make sense to agree to a payment plan and still get sued for the full amount and still have a judgment against you. Also, **do not agree to have the overall case just "settled."** If you do, it will still show up on your credit report as a negative mark. You want the case to be completely dropped so that your credit report will be unaffected; therefore the lawyers must agree on **"Voluntarily Withdrawn" or "dismissed" by the creditors.**

If you already have a judgment there are still things that you can do. You can always **pay it off** if possible but it will still show up on your report. You can also **have the judgment Vacated if there is a defe**ct in the lawsuit. If something was entered incorrectly or in error you can use that as grounds to remove the judgment. You can file a motion in the same court where the judgment was entered against you. Here are a few reasons you can use in your defense:

1.   **You do not know or never heard of the creditor.**
2.   **The amount of the judgment entered is incorrect.**
3.   **You did not see the paper or court summons due to an illness, being out of town, a death in the family, relocation to a new address, etc.**
4.   **The creditor did not follow the proper notification rules and guidelines.**
5.   **Have the CRAs confirm the accuracy of the judgment.**

The best thing to do is to not let the judgment reach your report. You will be surprised to know that many creditors would be willing to work with you during a hardship.

Communication is the key so don't be intimidated or afraid to pick up the phone and tell them the truth about your situation. You never know what the person on the other end can do for you. It is when you stop communicating and ignore the commitment that things will get bad for you.

Now it is not a guarantee that these techniques or strategies will work but based off past experiences, you have a really good chance of getting a better result than if you just ignore it. You cannot run from your credit or your debt and you honestly shouldn't want to. Your credit can create a world of opportunity for you if you take care of it.

Furthermore, there are settlement letters to be found online to help you out. Be sure to contact the lawyers of the creditors, negotiate a **"Pay for Removal"**, make your offer, and see how things pan out. **Remember that the order must be vacated and not just settled.** Ask that all negative markings be removed from your credit report.

DIVORCE AFTERMATH

When two people come together in marriage and decide to share their lives together, it can be a beautiful thing. Almost everyone out there wishes for their fairytale romance. Unfortunately, life is not always so sweet and divorce is a serious possibility for many couples. 75% of divorces are due to financial problems.

Going through a divorce can be a strenuous and difficult process emotionally, mentally, and especially, financially. To illustrate how a divorce can impact two individuals financially, let's read about Mr. and Mrs. Smith.

Mr. and Mrs. Smith started off as quite the happy couple. Mr. Smith was a successful contractor and Mrs. Smith was happy with her career as a school teacher. However, after years of stress in their relationship – Mr. Smith works too much and is less than romantic, Mrs. Smith doesn't work enough, always shopping, etc. –

they decide to call it quits. They file for the divorce and the judge proceeds to divide their assets. Mr. Smith gets the car and Mrs. Smith gets the house. Mr. Smith must pay for both the car and the house mortgage while Mrs. Smith must pay off their three maxed out credit cards.

Let's pause this story for a while and ask a simple question: why do people find themselves in debt and with bad credit after a divorce?

Looking at Mr. and Mrs. Smith it is quite easy to answer that question. To begin, Mr. Smith now has more things to pay for all on his own: the house, the car, and his new apartment because mom isn't letting him move in. Also, if you were to ask Mr. Smith who is responsible for the credit cards, he would say Mrs. Smith. On the other hand if you were to ask Mrs. Smith who is responsible for the car and mortgage, she would say Mr. Smith. Both of their answers are wrong.

After a divorce, if precautions are not taken, the credit score of both parties can be severely damaged. Although the divorce allowed them to both go their separate ways, it has nothing to do with what they did while they were married. They both signed for the house, the car, the credit cards, etc. Therefore the creditors can come after both Mr. and Mrs. Smith even after the divorce. So if Mr. Smith misses payments on the mortgage, Mrs. Smith can be held accountable. The negative marking that will appear on Mr. Smith's credit report will also be reflected on Mrs. Smith's credit report. **The divorce courts have no power over the creditors.**

This can be quite a problem but fortunately there are some solutions depending on where you are in the divorce process: married with no petition filed, married with a petition filed but not yet granted, or divorced.

If you are still married then you have quite a few options available to you that will keep your credit score looking healthy. The first thing to do, of course, is to gather information regarding all of your accounts, expenses, loans, etc. Also try to get a current copy of your credit report. Look over all of these documents to see which items have you and your spouse are both liable for the payments. Also make sure that all accounts are being paid on time and have no missing payments on their history.

The next thing I would suggest that you do is to get a credit card in your name only. This will allow you to build up good credit both before and after the divorce. If you wait until after the divorce, getting approved for a credit card may become more difficult. If you cannot get a credit card in your name because of bad credit or no credit, look into getting a low limit credit card or consider getting an installment loan or a secured card. If you can get an installment loan for about $500 and then just pay it off in a few months, you can definitely establish some good credit in a short period of time.

My next piece of advice is to close any joint accounts that you have with your spouse. This can be easy in some cases and difficult in others. If you both have a credit card together that has a balance of $0, then asking your creditor to close the account will be no problem. However, if the credit card has an existing balance on it, no amount of begging will get the creditor to close the account until the balance is paid off. If you don't have the cash to pay off existing balances you can try to open up two individual accounts and have the balance split equally and transferred over. With the smaller secured loans, you can either pay them off or refinance them under one of your names. You can do the same thing with the mortgage or you can sell it in order to remove joint liability for the account. Now, if for some reason your home is **"underwater," meaning you owe more on the property than what it is actually worth, there are programs available to help you.** Contact your mortgage company for more information. Divorces can be pretty messy but if you have the opportunity to work with your spouse before the divorce to get these things done, you both will benefit in the long run.

For those of you who are in the middle of a divorce, things can be a bit trickier. As stated before, try to close all joint accounts. Also, you can write to the creditor and ask that the accounts with a balance be frozen. This will not get rid of the existing balance or close the account but it will prevent any further charges from being made on the account. As far as the mortgage is concerned, consider refinancing. If the spouse keeping the house can afford to refinance on his or her own, then great. If that isn't possible due to weak credit, then try to refinance together to lower the payment amount. Lowering the payment increases the chance that the mortgage will actually get paid. If the person keeping the home will not be able to afford the payments, his or her credit rating can be quickly damaged. At this point, one of you can deed over the interest of the home so that selling the house can be an option.

If you are already divorced and your credit hasn't taken too much damage, there are still some things you can do to make sure that your credit stays undamaged. Once again, make sure to freeze any accounts. As far as property such as cars and houses are concerned, refinance them separately and be sure to ask your spouse to sign over the interest so they are no longer held liable. You want to be sure that all payments are being made on time so get copies of all invoices for the accounts still held jointly. Even if you are not responsible for the payments you have a right to the invoices.

If you are divorced but your credit is damaged, there are ways to repair it. Whatever the reasons for your damaged credit, following the advice given in the previous chapters will surely get you back on track.

TIPS OF THE TRADE

We have covered quite a bit of information and I introduced a lot of tips and advice therefore I just want to use this chapter as sort of a summary. I will also introduce some miscellaneous pieces of advice that I hope will prove to be useful. I have ten tips that I hope you will apply and remember.

1. **Check your credit report at least once a year** but try to do it twice if possible. Almost **4 out of 5 credit reports will have an error** listed on it that can impact your score negatively and dramatically. Checking your report for inaccuracies can mean the difference between getting a new car and suffering through outrageous interest rates. It also allows for

disputes to be raised which can lead to the inaccuracies being removed. **Identity theft is another important reason to check your report.** Which brings me to the second tip;

2.   **Get Identity Theft Protection.** Identity theft, surprisingly, occurs often and can cause a lot of distress and trouble if you are a victim of it. Your credit can be damaged extensively and your financial wellbeing can be in jeopardy if you are a victim. Some people lose everything: their house, car, savings, etc. Therefore protecting yourself is important.

3.   **Always pay more than the minimum payment on your credit cards** otherwise you will be in debt for a very long time. Paying more than the minimum payment will also save you money on interest. If you have a balance of $100 and your minimum payment is $15, try paying $25 or $50 if possible. Practice this strategy until it becomes second nature.

4.   REMINDER: **Keep your credit card balances below 30%.** Usage is a big factor in calculating your credit score and keeping your usage low will save you some money on interest and keep your credit score looking good.

5.   **Pay all of your debts before the reporting date. This is more of a little credit secret although it is a tip too.**

The reporting date is the day that the creditors report the balance owed on the account to the CRAs. You will have a "bill due" date and then the **"reporting date"**. The sneaky part is that the bill due date is not always before the reporting date. Having a balance on your account when it is reported can cost you points on your credit score.

6.   REMINDER: **Keep older accounts open** and certainly do not close your old accounts. And if you only have one account, **do not close it.** If you have too many accounts, close the newer ones first. Let the older accounts continue to age like fine wine.

7.   This tip is a little bit tricky because I am all for helping people out, especially if they are in serious need. With that being said, even though I may feel a bit bad about this, **do not cosign for anyone or let anyone use your credit.** When it comes to your credit nobody is going to respect it the way you do. When you cosign for a loan you become just as responsible as the person you are helping out. If that person stops making payments, guess who has to make them or risk credit damage...You. So unless you are ready to take on the full responsibility of making the payments, I would not recommend cosigning for anyone: mom, dad, daughter, sister, best friend even significant other, not even granny. Sorry grandma.

8. **Do not use credit for everyday expenses.** I see so many people do this but it is not a good idea. Why pay interest rates for buying laundry detergent and milk? Don't increase your daily living expenses with interest unless under dire (and I mean DIRE!) circumstances.

9. **Use your credit to create opportunities and not debt.** Consider buying a property below market value and then selling it for a greater profit. That would be using your credit in a way that will gain you money.

10. **TEACH THE KIDS!** I cannot stress this enough. The children are our future, our legacy. Help them and guide them to a debt free and financially healthy future.
You have the knowledge of credit and that gives you power. Now give it to the kids and watch the generations harness that power into something great.
Follow these tips. **Read and reread this book.** Read other books too. Either way, I just want you to gain the knowledge necessary to take control of your credit and your finances.

At this moment **"You have the power!"**

WITH GREAT POWER COMES GREAT RESPONSIBILITY

Well there it is.

You have come to the end of the book and you have been granted a **Power** that you can harness into a **Superpower.** You can become your own superhero and perhaps somebody else's. You can save not only your credit, but your happiness. The sky is the limit when it comes to credit and you can now be free to soar. I surely hope your credit score will fly along with you and reach the levels that only a lucky few have been able to attain. Perfect credit is no longer a figment of your imagination but rather a reasonable and obtainable goal.

I wrote this book to teach you some technical terms regarding credit but I mostly wrote this book in a way that you could understand and relate to. I truly want people to know about the **Gem that is Credit** and how to treasure it so that financial hardships may be minimized and pass you by. The fact that we aren't taught about credit in our youth should be considered a crime. Letting others benefit from our ignorance is no longer going to happen. Take this book for what it is worth and take its knowledge and message to heart. It is up to us as our own person to make a change in our lives, for better or for worse.

I would like to thank everybody who has made this book possible and I give a warm thanks to all of those who have picked up this book and read it. I truly hope that the simple yet effective advice I have shared will change your life for the better. I wish you all peace, love, happiness, and prosperity. I pray and wish that all of your goals and dreams come true.

Thank You.

-T. Santos

CREDIT RESOURCES

THE POWER OF CREDIT
PUBLISHING
POWEROFCREDIT.COM

Sample Dispute Letter

Date:

Name of Credit Bureau

Address of Credit Bureau

City, State, Zip

To Whom It May Concern:

I am requesting that the following inaccurate items on my credit report be investigated immediately. They must be removed so that my true credit history can accurately be reflected. These items do not belong on my credit report. Pursuant to the Fair Credit Reporting Act, I will expect to have the results of the investigation within thirty days.

Company Name	Account number	Comments
1.		
2.		

Please send me my updated credit report upon completion of your investigation.

Sincerely,

Your, Signature

Full Name

Address

Social Security Number

Date of Birth

Sample Goodwill Letter

Date:

Name of Credit Bureau

Address of Credit Bureau

City, State, Zip

To Whom It May Concern:

I am writing this letter in hope of getting some assistance with account number. I am hoping to have an adjustment made out of "Goodwill" on my credit report regarding the late payments that were made on this account. I take full responsibility for my actions. At the time of the late payments I was experiencing a financial hardship and since then I have been consistent with my payment obligations with the company.

I am a loyal satisfied customer with the company and will continue to be long into the future. Based on my past and current payment history it shows that outside of this time period I have always made my payments on time. I would greatly appreciate it if you would consider removing the negative marking that are being report to the credit bureaus. I look forward to hearing back from you as soon as you have made your decision. Thank you so much for your attention to this matter at it is of great importance to me.

Sincerely,

Name:

Address:

Phone number:

Credit Reporting Agencies

If for some reason you need to contact the Credit Bureaus I have provided their contact information below. Feel free to call them with any of your questions comments or concerns as they are more than willing to help. I have used their numbers many times and have received great service and results each time. **Also visit their websites as they are extremely helpful and it is there that you may dispute items on your credit report online, which is a great option to have at your fingertips.**

TransUnion Consumer Relations
PO Box 1000
Chester, PA 19022
(800) 916-8800
www.transunion.com

Equifax Consumer Relations
PO Box 740241
Atlanta, GA 30374
(800) 685-1111
www.equifax.com

Experian Consumer Relations
PO Box 2002
Allen, TX 75013
(888) 397-3742
www.experian.com

Power of Credit Services

www.PowerofCredit.com

Credit Education

Clients are provided with the basic knowledge needed to understand their personal credit and reach their credit goals. Clients are taught how to accurately read and comprehend their credit report and how to properly manage their credit accounts. Information from the Fair Credit Reporting Act (abbr. FCRA) is provided in order to enlighten clients of the rights associated with their credit. Clients are also taught key components used to calculate their FICO Credit score so that they can achieve a respectable credit rating. The goal of the Education Service is to provide clients with the knowledge to change their credit and financial well-being for the best.

Credit Improvement and Enhancement

Through this service using a customized credit program designed for the client's personal credit we are able to improve the client's credit rating. Negative items that may be inaccurate, outdated, filed in error, or unverifiable are removed from the credit report. We use proven strategies to raise the credit score and structuring the credit file in a way that appeals to most lenders. Clients are also provided with options to enhance their personal credit rating by several points in a short period of time.

Credit Enhancement services are especially valuable to those clients who are seeking to make a big purchase such as a home, automobile etc. Through this service clients are also taught one of the credit industries best kept secrets.

Credit Building

Through this service clients are provided programs that will help to establish or re-establish their credit. Clients with little to no credit history are exposed to different programs that will aid them in beginning a strong and healthy credit file. Clients who need to rebuild or start all over are shown options that will allow them to get their credit back on the right track.

Debt Consultation

This service provides clients with the best possible solutions available to help them deal with their debt. After analyzing the clients debt, a strategic, customized program is created that will help to eliminate the negative debt forever. We also aid the client in negotiating possible settlements with the creditors. Clients are also aided in prioritizing their debt and creating an order of importance in dealing with their debt. Clients are also educated on the difference between good debt, bad debt and much more.

Credit Speaking Engagements

Through this service we give up to a forty five minute presentation on credit. Topics covered include but are not limited to; the importance of credit, how to properly manage your credit profile, how to maximize your credit rating, how to build, rebuild and enhance your credit rating and much more.

NOTES
SECTION

Made in the USA
San Bernardino, CA
20 January 2015